PEDALING ALONG

BIKES THEN AND NOW

PEDALING ALONG

BIKES THEN AND NOW

Steve Otfinoski

BENCHMARK BOOKS

MARSHALL CAVENDISH
NEW YORK

Benchmark Books
Marshall Cavendish Corporation
99 White Plains Road
Tarrytown, New York 10591-9001

Library of Congress-in-Publication Data
Otfinoski, Steven.
Pedaling along : bikes then and now / by Steven Otfinoski.
     p.   cm. — (Here we go!)
Includes bibliographical references and index.
ISBN 0-7614-0402-3 (lib. bdg.)
1. Bicycles—Juvenile literature. 2. Cycling—Juvenile
literature. I. Title. II. Series: Here we go!
TL410.086   1997   629.227'2—dc20   96-1136   CIP   AC

Photo research by Matthew Dudley

Cover photo: Photo Researchers, Inc./Tim Davis

The photographs in this book are used by permission and through the
courtesy of: *The Image Bank:* Gary Crallé, 1; Fracisco Hidalgo, 18(top);
Giuliano Colliva, 18-19; J. Mahaux, 20(center); John Kelly, 25, 27(bottom).
Photo Researchers, Inc.: George Haling, 2; Jean-Yves Ruszniewski, 6;
Jim Corwin, 16; Bill Bachman, 17(top left); Rita Nannini, 17(top right);
Tim Davis, 17(bottom), 30; Gaillard/Jerrican, 26(left); J. Tisne, 28-29;
John Clare du Bois, back cover. *Corbis-Bettmann:* 3, 7, 8, 9(top & bottom),
10, 11, 12, 13(top & bottom), 15, 22-23. *General Research Division,
New York Public Library, Astor, Lenox and Tilden Foundations:* 14.
FPG International Corp.: Telegraph Colour Library, 18(bottom left);
Dennie Cody, 20-21; Josef Beck, 21(center); Scott Markewitz, 26(right),
27(top); Michael Hart, 32. *Reuters/Corbis- Bettmann:* 21(right), 24.
Frans Stoppelman: 20(left).

Printed and bound in the United States

6   5   4   3   2

To Martha, one wild kid on wheels

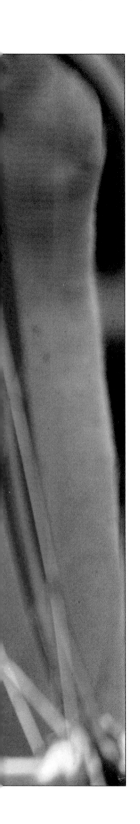

*J*ust imagine for a moment you're riding your bike.
You're pedaling like mad up a hill.
You reach the top and start down.
You're going faster and faster.
The wind is blowing in your face.
Trees and houses whiz by you.
What could be more thrilling?
People have been enjoying bicycling for a long time.
Bikes have been around longer than trains and cars and motorcycles.
Let's pedal back in time and see how it all started.

The man who invented the first modern bicycle
was a German official.
His name was Baron Karl Von Drais.
He had to walk the countryside in his job.
The baron invented his bicycle so he could get around easier.
The "Draisine," as it was called, had no pedals,
no brakes, and no gears.
You had to push it along the ground with your feet.
Going downhill was fun, but walking it back uphill
was hard work.

Some people improved on
the baron's bike.
But bikes were still pretty
strange looking,
like the one this girl is riding.
The bike to the left has pedals.
But the wheels and seat
are made of iron.
It was called a "boneshaker."
Can you guess why?

9

Bikes became very popular.
People went to special schools
to learn how to ride a bicycle.
It wasn't easy!

The 1890s was the Golden Age of Bicycle Riding.
People rode bikes to work. They raced bikes for sport.
They dressed up and rode bikes on Sunday
afternoons in the park.
Bikes took people to new and exciting places.
But kids didn't ride bikes back then.
They were too big, too hard to ride, and too expensive!

Not everyone liked bikes.
Some people said they were dangerous
because they went so fast.
Police arrested bikers for speeding.
But that didn't stop people from riding
bicycles in all shapes and sizes.

Some bicyclists became heroes.

Thomas Stevens went across America on a high-wheel bike.

He faced many dangers along the way.

The next year he went around the world.
He pedaled across Europe...

and Asia, and then sailed back to America.

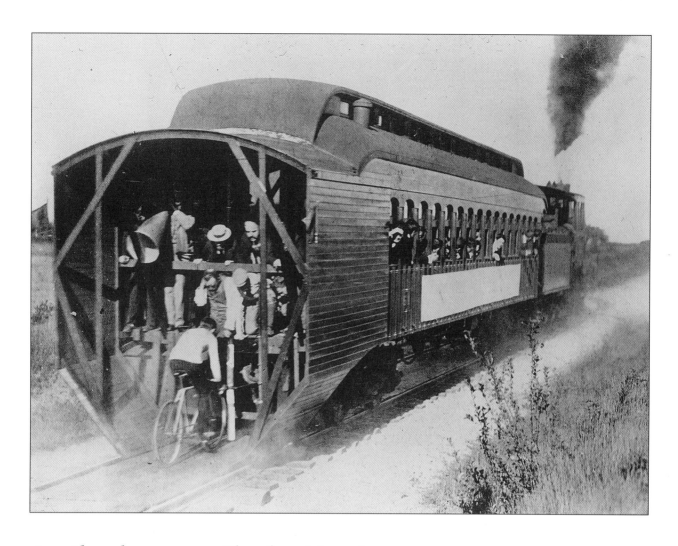

Another hero was Charles Murphy.
He claimed he could pedal his bike
as fast as a train.
One railroad challenged him to a race.
Murphy reached a top speed of sixty miles an hour
and won.
After that, they called him "Mile-a-Minute" Murphy.

But then people found a new invention
to take them places.
It was called the automobile.
After that, only children rode bicycles.

Little kids rode tricycles
with three wheels.
Bigger kids rode bikes
with tiny training wheels
to help them keep their balance.
The biggest kids rode bikes
with only two wheels.

In other countries, as many adults ride bikes
as children do.
In countries like China and India there are more
bicycles than cars.
People ride bikes to work and to school.
Bike "taxis" take people wherever they want to go.

In big cities, workers ride around on bicycles.
Some carry the news.
Others carry messages from one part of the
city to another.
They whiz through the busy traffic
faster than any car.

Bikes are used to carry goods as well as people
in many countries.
No load is too big for a bike!

These bikers are racing in the Tour de France. It is the most famous bicycle race in the world.

In the 1960s many Americans
rediscovered bicycle riding.
They found riding bikes
was good exercise.
And bikes didn't pollute
the air like cars and
other vehicles.
New bikes were easier to ride, too.
They were built for speed
and made for racing.
Today bike racing is
a big sport in many countries.
Some races have hundreds of bikers
and last for days.

Racing bikes are built for speed.
The racers wear tight-fitting uniforms
and sturdy helmets.
They race on special streamlined tracks,
indoors and outdoors.
The fastest bike ever reached a speed
of 127 miles per hour.
That's faster than most cars can go!

Some bikes are built to go
almost anywhere on earth.
They have wide, sturdy tires
and light, rugged frames.
They can travel through
water and mud.

They can climb up
and down mountains.
Bikes can even go through
ice and snow.

Bicycles have been around a long time.
They will be around as long as people
are looking for adventure—
whether it's around the world
or just down the block.
As one writer put it many years ago,
"Just straddle a saddle,
then paddle and skedaddle."
In other words,
Keep pedaling along!

FIND OUT MORE

Henkel, Stephen C. *Bikes.* New York: Chattam Press, 1972.

Loeper, John F. *Away We Go! On Bicycles in 1898.* New York: Atheneum, 1982.

Rockwell, Anne. *Bikes.* New York: Puffin Books, 1991.

Be a responsible biker rider. Always wear a helmet!

INDEX

STEVE OTFINOSKI has written more than sixty books for children. He also has a theater company called *History Alive!* that performs plays for schools about people and events from the past. Steve lives in Stratford, Connecticut, with his wife and two children.